WITHDRAWN

Capybaras

Leo Statts

abdopublishing.com

Published by Abdo Zoom™, PO Box 398166, Minneapolis, Minnesota 55439. Copyright © 2017 by Abdo Consulting Group, Inc. International copyrights reserved in all countries. No part of this book may be reproduced in any form without written permission from the publisher. Abdo Zoom™ is a trademark and logo of Abdo Consulting Group, Inc.

Printed in the United States of America, North Mankato, Minnesota
062016
092016

Cover Photo: Vladislav T. Jirousek/Shutterstock Images
Interior Photos: iStockphoto, 1, 6, 8, 8–9; Shutterstock Images, 4–5, 18–19; Scott McClure/iStockphoto, 7; Vadim Petrakov/Shutterstock Images, 10–11, 12–13; Red Line Editorial, 11, 20 (left), 20 (right), 21 (left), 21 (right); Jan Gottwald/iStockphoto, 15; Bruno Vieira/Shutterstock Images, 16; Edwin Butter/Shutterstock Images, 18

Editor: Brienna Rossiter
Series Designer: Madeline Berger
Art Direction: Dorothy Toth

Publisher's Cataloging-in-Publication Data
Names: Statts, Leo, author.
Title: Capybaras / by Leo Statts.
Description: Minneapolis, MN : Abdo Zoom, [2017] | Series: Swamp animals |
    Includes bibliographical references and index.
Identifiers: LCCN 2016941157 | ISBN 9781680792072 (lib. bdg.) |
    ISBN 9781680793758 (ebook) | ISBN 9781680794649 (Read-to-me ebook)
Subjects: LCSH: Capybaras--Juvenile literature.
Classification: DDC 599.354--dc23
LC record available at http://lccn.loc.gov/2016941157

Table of Contents

Capybaras

Capybaras are the largest **rodents**. They have round bodies. Their fur is reddish brown.

Body

A capybara's eyes are near the top of its head. So are its ears and nostrils.

This allows it to spend lots of time in the water.

Capybaras have short legs.

Their feet are partly webbed.
This helps them swim.

Habitat

Capybaras live in South America.
They live in groups.
They are often found near water.

Where capybaras live

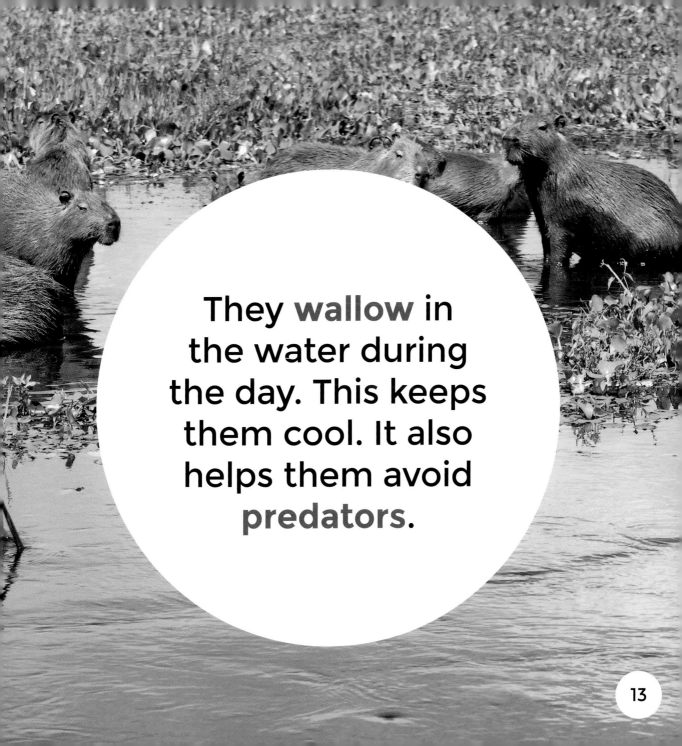

They **wallow** in the water during the day. This keeps them cool. It also helps them avoid **predators**.

Food

Capybaras eat lots of grass.
They **gnaw** their food.
Their front teeth never
stop growing.

Life Cycle

A female capybara leaves the group to give birth. She returns with the babies.

All the females in the group help raise the babies.

Capybaras live about eight years.

Average Length

A capybara is about as long as an acoustic guitar.

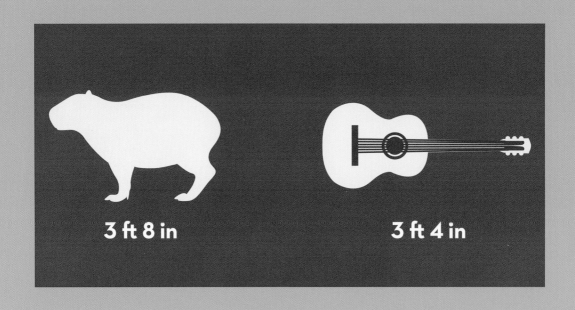

3 ft 8 in   3 ft 4 in

Average Weight

A capybara is heavier
than a toilet.

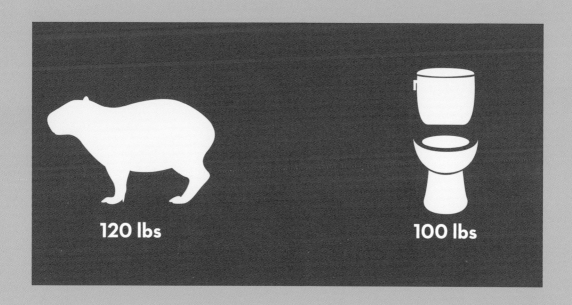

120 lbs   100 lbs

Glossary

gnaw - to wear down with tiny bites.

predator - an animal that hunts others.

rodent - a small animal with large front teeth.

wallow - to roll about in a lazy or relaxed way.

webbed - joined together by skin, like the toes of a duck or frog.

Booklinks

For more information
on **capybaras**, please visit
booklinks.abdopublishing.com

Zoom™ In on Animals!

Learn even more with the Abdo Zoom
Animals database. Check out
abdozoom.com for more information.

Index